LEADING LADY

NANCY REAGAN

Written by:
Jill Wheeler

Published by Abdo & Daughters, 6535 Cecilia Circle, Edina, Minnesota 55439.

Library bound edition distributed by Rockbottom Books, Pentagon Tower, P.O. Box 36036, Minneapolis, Minnesota 55435.

Library of Congress Number: 91-073027   ISBN: 1-56239-080-5

Photos by: Pictorial Parade

Edited by: Rosemary Wallner

TABLE OF CONTENTS

3

Former first lady, Nancy Reagan, with husband former President Ronald Reagan.

FIRST CLASS FIRST LADY

Former first lady Nancy Reagan was in the national spotlight from 1981-1989 during the presidency of her husband, Ronald Reagan. Even today, she and her husband are celebrities, attending parties, making speeches, and entertaining at their home in Bel Air, California.

"When Ronnie and I moved to Washington in 1981, I never dreamed that our eight years there would be a time of so much emotion," she said. "Life in the White House is magnified: The highs were higher than I expected, and the lows were much lower."

Reagan has come a long way since her first days in the White House. Early in her husband's first term, she was criticized for spending $800,000 on redecorating her family's White House living quarters. The project was paid for with private donations, but many people thought it was wrong to spend money on decorating when many Americans were losing their jobs. Some members of the press referred to her as "Queen Nancy, the Belle of Rodeo Drive," after the expensive shopping area in Beverly Hills, California.

"The first year was a terrible year," Reagan recalled. "From the beginning, I was certainly aware that everybody was not just cuckoo about me."

As the years passed, Reagan became more sure of herself and learned to live in the public eye. When she began her work to fight drug abuse, she won the respect of many people. Throughout her time as first lady, she believed her primary role was to guard her husband's health and his reputation. Other than that personal desire, she had no job description to guide her.

"Everybody who's been here knows the job's tough," she said of life in the White House. "Nothing – nothing – prepares you for being first lady."

UNHAPPY BEGINNINGS

Nancy Reagan was born Anne Frances Robbins on July 6, 1921, in New York City. Her parents, car salesman Kenneth Robbins and actress Edith "Lucky" Luckett, separated later that year. Young Anne, who soon received the nickname Nancy, became a backstage baby, traveling with her mother as Edith pursued her acting career.

When Nancy was two years old, her mother sent her to Maryland to live with Edith's sister's family. "It was a painful period for both of us," Reagan recalled. "I missed her terribly. No matter how kindly you are treated, and I was treated with great love, your mother is your mother and nobody else can ever fill that role in your life."

Reagan's aunt and uncle had a daughter of their own, Reagan's cousin Charlotte. The two girls were treated equally. Reagan's aunt and uncle sent the two girls to Sidwell Friends School, an expensive private school in Washington, D.C. There, Reagan made friends with the children of some of the nation's most influential people at the time. She quickly adapted to the Washington lifestyle and enjoyed spending time with her new friends.

Reagan's mother visited her daughter when she could. Occasionally, Reagan visited Edith in New York and watched her perform. She was too young to realize her mother was just acting. "She was in a play... in which they were very mean to her," Reagan remembered. "And I got so upset that, sitting up there in a box, watching, I began to cry. I guess I created quite a commotion."

THE FAIRY TALE BEGINS

Things changed dramatically in the spring of 1929 when Edith married Chicago surgeon Dr. Loyal Davis and brought Nancy to live with them in Chicago. "It was like a happy ending to a fairy tale," Reagan said of her mother's remarriage. "I really couldn't have asked for a more wonderful father."

That fall, the stock market crashed, sending the nation into the Great Depression. While millions of Americans went hungry, Reagan and her family enjoyed big dinners, fancy clothes, and parties. Reagan and her half-brother, Richard Davis, spent many hours entertaining their mother's acting friends, including Spencer Tracy, Lillian Gish, and Walter Huston. Being around actors encouraged the two children to make up their own plays during the family's summer vacations.

Reagan attended school at the exclusive Girls Latin School in Chicago. When she was 14 years old, she was legally adopted by her stepfather. She proudly told her classmates they could call her Nancy Davis.

At Girls Latin School, Reagan was poised, perfectly groomed, and sociable. She was involved in many school organizations, including the hockey team, glee club, and student government. She also played the title role in her senior class play, *The First Lady*.

Following graduation she enrolled at Smith College in Massachusetts where she studied English and drama. After graduating from Smith in 1943, she worked for a while in a Chicago department store, then moved to New York to pursue an acting career on Broadway. Thanks to her mother's ties in the theater world, she met Clark Gable during her time in New York. The two spent a week together before Gable returned to Hollywood.

HOLLYWOOD STARLET

Eventually, Reagan also moved to Hollywood where she signed an acting contract with Metro-Goldwyn-Mayer studios and began making movies. One day in 1949, she saw her name in a Hollywood paper on a list of Communist sympathizers.

In the 1940s, people were afraid of Russian Communists. If someone's name appeared on a list of sympathizers, that person was often shunned and feared. Reagan was concerned about seeing her name on the list. Other actors urged her to contact the president of the Screen Actors Guild, a handsome young actor named Ronald Reagan. They told her he would be able to help her.

"I don't know exactly if it was love at first sight, but it was pretty close," Reagan said about her first meeting with Ronald. "I have never doubted for one single instant that Ronnie and I belonged together." She also discovered upon meeting Ronald Reagan that there were at least three women in Hollywood named Nancy Davis. Probably, Ronald Reagan told her, it was a different Nancy Davis whose name was on the list in the newspaper.

After dating for more than two years, Nancy and Ronald were married on March 4, 1952. By that time she had made eight movies. She continued to act even after the birth of their first daughter, Patti. She also had the opportunity to star opposite her husband in the movie *Hellcats of the Navy*. Reagan had stopped acting by the time their son, Ron Jr., was born in 1958, although she and her husband made one final film together in 1960.

Ronald Reagan and then Nancy Davis were both Hollywood stars in the 1950s.

ON TO SACRAMENTO

After she quit acting, Reagan devoted herself to being a full-time wife and mother. In addition to her two children, she sometimes took care of her husband's children from his earlier marriage to actress Jane Wyman. Their names were Maureen and Michael Reagan.

In her spare time, Reagan became active in a social group called the Colleagues. She made friends with many of the members while helping the group hold fund-raisers for charity. Some of the women she met in the Colleagues have been her good friends ever since.

Meanwhile, Reagan's husband was phasing out his acting career and becoming involved in politics. He made his first big splash on the political scene in 1964 with a nationally televised fund-raising speech for Republican presidential candidate Barry Goldwater. After hearing the speech, many people urged him to run for governor of California. He did so in 1966 and won the election. The Reagan family's next move was to Sacramento, the capital of California.

After marrying Ronald Reagan, Nancy quit acting and became a full-time housewife.

While Reagan had helped her husband campaign
for governor, she found her new political life very
different from life as a Hollywood actress. "Politics
is a completely different life," she said. "In the
picture business you're protected somewhat. In
politics you aren't protected in any way."

Reagan was not happy in Sacramento at first.
She did not know many people in the area, so
she devoted herself to taking care of her husband.
She had his office redecorated then, with the
help of her friends in Los Angeles, she redeco-

rated their home. On weekends, the couple frequently traveled to Los Angeles to visit friends.

While first lady of California, Reagan became involved in the Foster Grandparents program. Foster Grandparents matches older volunteers with orphaned or disabled children. She also spent many hours volunteering her time at hospitals cheering the patients. In Los Angeles, she shopped and had lunch with her friends. She became known as a trendsetter in the fashion world.

Talk soon turned to Ronald Reagan as a presidential candidate. Reagan was not pleased at the idea of her husband as president, although she believed he would do the job well. She was surprised one day when she heard on the radio that he had decided to run for the Republican presidential nomination. It was the first and last major political decision he ever made without consulting her.

Ronald Reagan was unsuccessful in his bid for the 1968 presidential nomination, losing to another Californian, Richard Nixon. He lost the nomination again in 1976 to Gerald Ford. But in 1980, the timing was right. He was elected president of the United States in a landslide victory.

FINALLY – WASHINGTON

Ronald and Nancy Reagan moved to Washington, D.C. in early 1981 for the $16 million presidential inauguration, the most expensive in the history of the nation. As the gala events wound down, Reagan began adjusting to her new role as the nation's first lady. "It was so new to me," she said of her position. "I didn't know quite what to do, and there's no training for this job."

Suddenly Reagan had a staff of 17 people and a budget of half a million dollars. She decided her first project would be to redecorate the family's living quarters in the White House. While each president received $50,000 for redecorating, Reagan knew it would take more than that to do what she wanted. Thanks to donations from friends, she was able to hire her favorite decorator and get the rooms in order for about $800,000.

Many people criticized Reagan for her expensive tastes in decorating, as well as her clothing. They were upset she was wearing $10,000 dresses when so many of her fellow Americans were without jobs. Reagan tried to explain that the money for redecorating, along with many of her clothes, had been donated, but the criticism continued.

Reagan was deeply hurt by people's views on her lifestyle. Then in March 1981, her life became even more complicated when her husband was wounded in an assassination attempt. "It was a nightmare," she said of the incident. "I still wake up at night remembering that scene (in the hospital)."

The stress of being ridiculed by the public and almost losing her husband made 1981 a very difficult year for Reagan. She lost weight, dropping to just 104 pounds, and became increasingly quiet and depressed. "My nature is to get quiet and pull back if something hurts or is bothering me," she said. "I pulled back from the press, for example, because I felt hurt and didn't give them a chance to know me."

That July, her husband asked her if she would like to represent the U.S. at the wedding of Britain's Prince Charles and Lady Diana Spencer. Reagan was delighted at the chance to attend the fairy tale wedding. Her husband hoped it would make her feel better after the difficult year she had had so far.

*President Reagan and wife Nancy visit with the
Prince of Wales and his soon-to-be princess, a week
before the royal wedding.*

Reagan flew to England with 20 staff members and friends, and more than 20 different dresses and gowns. During her week's visit, she attended parties, a polo match, dinners, and balls as well as the royal wedding. "I was overjoyed at the graciousness of the whole royal family," she said. "Altogether, this was a wonderful week."

A week after the royal wedding, Reagan and her husband left for a month-long vacation at their ranch in California. Upon returning, Reagan soon purchased more than $200,000 in new china with money donated by friends. She then allowed the prestigious magazine *Architectural Digest* to publish photographs of the newly redecorated White House. Once again, she became a target for criticism by members of the media.

Reagan won some of those hearts back the next spring with a surprise performance at the annual Gridiron dinner. The Gridiron is a group of 60 journalists who put on a special dinner for the president and top officials each year.

At the dinner, Reagan appeared in old, unmatched clothes and sang the song "Secondhand Clothes." Her performance was rewarded with a standing ovation. Shortly thereafter, she embarked on another campaign which earned her the respect of millions of people around the nation.

"JUST SAY NO"

As California's first lady, Reagan had been involved in volunteer work to help promote the Foster Grandparents program. In the White House, she turned her attention and energies to what she considered a more serious problem – drug abuse among young people.

"I always knew I wanted to be involved in the drug problem, and then I had more time," she said. "Drug abuse is a very serious problem – among youth, among working people... We do stand a chance of losing a whole generation to drugs. It's a very, very dangerous problem we're all facing."

Nancy Reagan got seriously involved in America's
drug prevention program — she coined the phrase
"Just say no."

Reagan's dedication to helping fight drug abuse led her to make hundreds of public appearances at schools and drug treatment centers. She played herself on a special episode of the television series "Diff'rent Strokes" and held an anti-drug forum with first ladies from around the globe. Her "Just Say No" to drugs campaign has been highly successful in drawing increased attention to the drug problem.

STRAINED FAMILY RELATIONS

Reagan had always presented a warm image to the public, but many times her smile hid her personal problems. Of particular trouble in her life had been her relationships with her children, Patti and Ron Jr., and her stepchildren, Maureen and Michael.

"Every family has problems, and we were no exception," Reagan admitted. "What I wanted most in all the world was to be a good wife and mother. As things turned out, I guess I've been more successful at the first than at the second."

From left to right: Patti Davis, Paul Grilley (Patti's husband), Nancy, Ronald Reagan, Doria Reagan, and Ron Reagan Jr.

Nancy Reagan with son, Ron Jr.

Like many parents, Reagan had a difficult time raising children during the late 1960s and 1970s. She was upset when Patti moved away to live with a member of a rock band. She also was hurt when Ron Jr. let his hair grow long, dropped out of Yale University, and became a professional dancer. She later accepted and even supported his career. She says she still hopes to become closer to Patti someday.

While Reagan had problems with her own children, they were not as severe as the problems she had with her husband's children. In 1981, Maureen Reagan ran for a Senate seat representing California but neither her father nor stepmother supported her campaign. Relations between the three have since improved.

Three years later, Michael Reagan complained publicly that his two-year-old daughter had never seen her grandfather. Shortly thereafter, the president and his wife met with Michael Reagan and his family at a Los Angeles hotel. After the meeting, Nancy Reagan said, "All is resolved. Everybody loves each other."

MEETING THE SOVIET UNION'S FIRST LADY

During Ronald Reagan's presidency, he made attempts to smooth relations between the U.S. and the Soviet Union. He arranged meetings with Soviet President Mikhail Gorbachev. It was only natural that the first ladies of the two nations should get together while their husbands met. Their first meeting was in 1985 in Geneva, Switzerland, when Reagan invited Raisa Gorbachev, the Soviet first lady, to tea at the house in which the Reagans were staying.

As Reagan recalls, the meeting was not a pleasant one. "That first tea in Geneva lasted slightly more than an hour," described Reagan. "There was a fire in the fireplace, but the conversation was dry, impersonal, and tedious. She was lecturing me about Communism, and I couldn't wait for her to stop."

The two first ladies met again in Washington, D.C., in December 1987 and again in Moscow in May 1988. While in Moscow, Reagan and Gorbachev toured an art gallery that contained a number of icons (religious images painted on wood). Reagan was late arriving at the gallery, so the tour had begun by the time she joined the rest of the people.

During the tour, a reporter said to Reagan that Gorbachev had told the people taking the tour that the icons had no religious significance. The reporter asked Reagan what she felt about that subject. "I don't know how you can neglect the religious implications," Reagan said. "I mean, they're there for everybody to see."

The people who witnessed the disagreement were quick to report that the two first ladies did not get along. However, in December 1988 when the two women met again in New York, Gorbachev told Reagan she hoped they would travel to the Soviet Union to visit again. Reagan quickly invited the Gorbachevs to visit California, as well.

"If Raisa and I had been left alone, without any press, we probably would have had an easier time of it," Reagan said. "But even before our first meeting in Geneva, there had been so much talk about the two of us that we were both enormously self-conscious. In any event, I'm very glad that we saw each other one last time in New York, which was a nice ending to a relationship that had obviously been difficult for both of us."

THE IRAN-CONTRA SCANDAL

As if the problems with Raisa Gorbachev were not enough, Reagan soon found herself in the middle of another difficult situation which became known as the Iran-Contra Scandal.

In November 1986, the media reported that the United States had sold $30 million worth of military equipment to Iran. Later it was learned some of the money from the sale had been given to the Contras, a rebel group fighting the government of Nicaragua. The Reagan Administration supported the efforts of the Contras, and President Reagan had asked Congress to give the Contras money. Many members of Congress and the public, however, did not agree with what the Contras were doing.

Most Americans were angry when they heard the news. Many thought the president was lying when he said he did not know about the sale and where the money went. Reagan was upset because she felt people were criticizing her husband unfairly. She blamed her husband's chief of staff, Donald Regan, for not knowing what was going on and not alerting the president to the situation.

Nancy Reagan and Regan had been at odds for many months. Their first disagreement occurred in 1985 after President Reagan's cancer surgery. The chief of staff wanted the president to meet with his advisers two days after his surgery. Reagan said it was too soon, and the president should be allowed more rest. Their problems continued after that. Regan believed Nancy Reagan interfered too much in her husband's business. Nancy Reagan believed Regan thought he was too powerful.

Reagan had often told her husband he should fire Regan. Now that the Iran-Contra Scandal had come to light, many other members of the Administration agreed. In March 1987, Regan resigned under pressure from many people, including Nancy Reagan.

Regan believed Nancy Reagan was the reason he was forced to resign. He blamed her for his downfall in a book he later wrote. Reagan disagreed. "If I were the dragon lady that he described in his book, he would have been out the door many months earlier," she said.

FIGHTING CANCER

It was October 1987, in the middle of her husband's second term as president, when Reagan learned she had breast cancer. Just two years earlier, her husband also had undergone surgery for colon cancer. As she wrote in her diary, "Cancer. There's something about the sound of that word which makes your heart stop."

She underwent surgery to remove her left breast. When she returned to the White House, staff members counted the number of cards and letters she had received. The total was more than 36,000. Less than ten days after her surgery, she learned that her mother had died of a stroke. Once again, misfortune followed misfortune.

THE ASTROLOGY PROBLEM

Things took another turn for the worse the next year when Donald Regan wrote a book on his days in the Reagan Administration. In his book, he said Reagan consulted an astrologer to help make the president's schedule. Astrology is the belief that the positions of the stars and planets can predict what will happen to a person.

Close friends of Reagan's say she began consulting the astrologer because she believed she could protect her husband from harm. According to her astrologer, the stars and planets had shown that late March 1981 was a dangerous time for President Reagan. The assassination attempt occurred on March 30, 1981.

Reagan defended her interest in astrology, saying it was only to help her husband. Ever since they were married, she had watched over him. She felt it was her most important job.

Nancy Reagan and President Ronald Reagan.

BACK TO CALIFORNIA

January 1989 saw the end of Ronald Reagan's second term as president. U.S. law prohibited him from running for president again, so the Reagans returned to Los Angeles.

Reagan said leaving the White House was a very emotional experience for the couple. "When we took off (in the helicopter), the pilots circled the White House so we could see it once more," she said. "This was really goodbye to Washington, and eight wonderful, exciting, frustrating, and sometimes frightening years."

The Reagans enjoy their new life out of the public eye and both remain active. Reagan continues to work against drug abuse through the Nancy Reagan Foundation and the Just Say No campaign. She is also glad to be able to lunch with her old Colleagues friends and reminisce about her experiences as the nation's first class first lady.